LATER ELEMENTARY TO EARLY INTERMEDIATE

STRANGE SOUNDS

ISBN 978-1-70514-920-1

EXCLUSIVELY DISTRIBUTED BY

WILLIS MUSIC

HAL•LEONARD®

Visit Hal Leonard Online at
www.halleonard.com

Contact us:
Hal Leonard
7777 West Bluemound Road
Milwaukee, WI 53213
Email: info@halleonard.com

In Europe, contact:
Hal Leonard Europe Limited
42 Wigmore Street
Marylebone, London, W1U 2RN
Email: info@halleonardeurope.com

In Australia, contact:
Hal Leonard Australia Pty. Ltd.
4 Lentara Court
Cheltenham, Victoria, 3192 Australia
Email: info@halleonard.com.au

Welcome to the world
of strange sounds.
The piano solos in this book may
be used for a Halloween recital,
or simply to stimulate
imaginations at any time
of the year.

CONTENTS

On This Eerie Night

Words and Music by
Glenda Austin

With trepidation

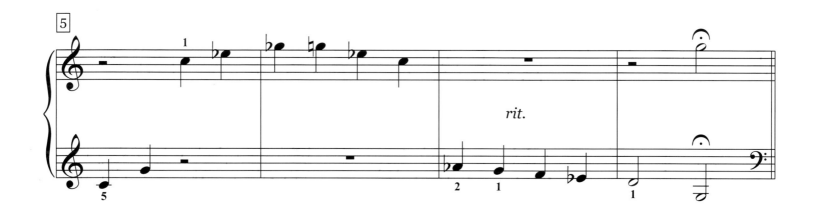

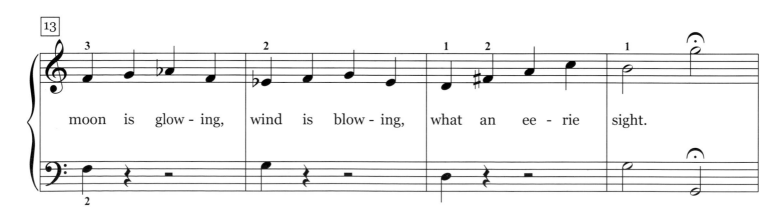

Spooks and ghouls ap - pear. There's no need to fear. So

rit.

rest as - sured, they're quite po - lite. No need __ to __ wor - ry __

a tempo

mp

on __ this __ ee - rie night!

mp

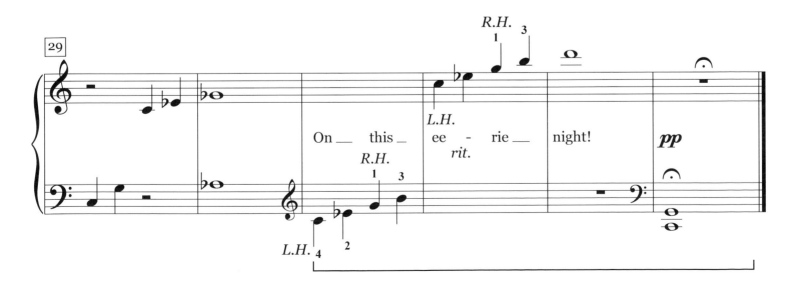

On __ this __ ee - rie __ night!

R.H.

L.H.

R.H.

rit.

L.H.

pp

Spooky Night

William Gillock

To Chris

A Haunted House

Words and Music by
Edna Mae Burnam

Very spooky

Rather slowly

Way out in the coun-try there's a haunt-ed house!

Way out in the coun-try there's a haunt-ed house!

It is scar-y there! Cob-webs ev-'ry-where!

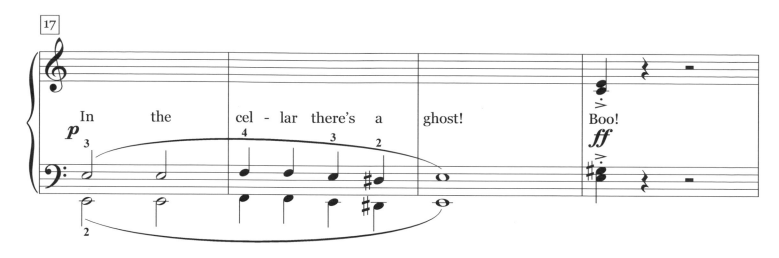

In the cel - lar there's a ghost! Boo!

Way out in the coun - try there's a haunt - ed house!

Way out in the coun - try there's a haunt - ed house!

29 A little faster

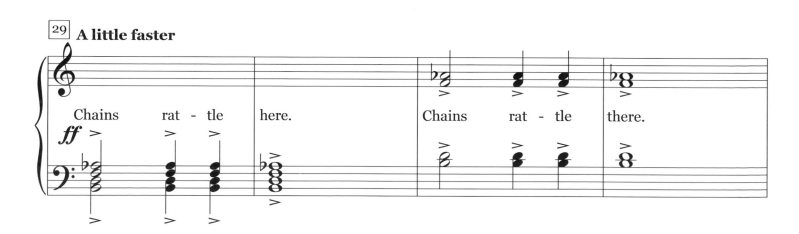

Chains rat - tle here. Chains rat - tle there.

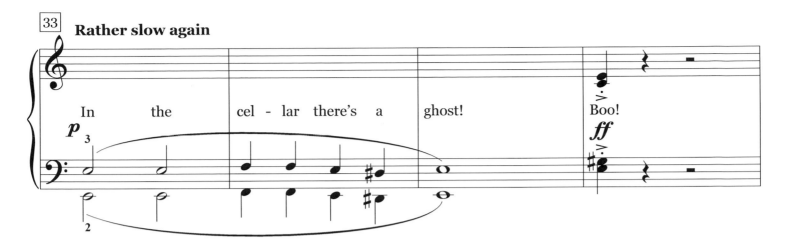

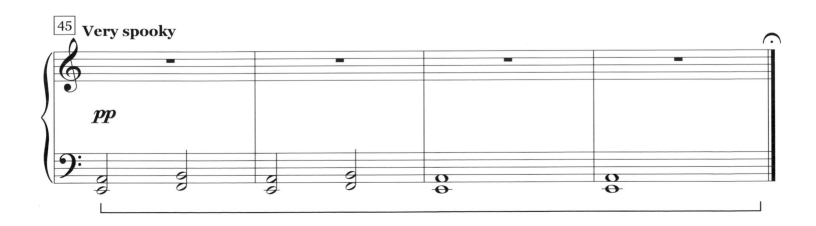

Escape from the Dark Forest

Randall Hartsell

Deviously

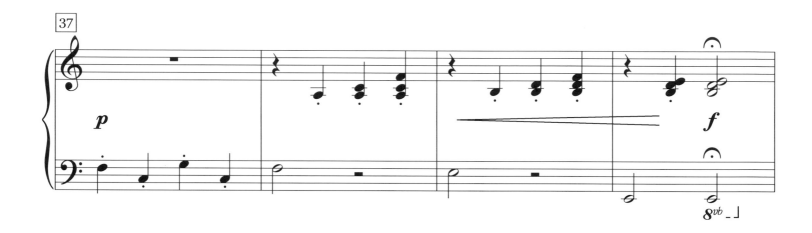

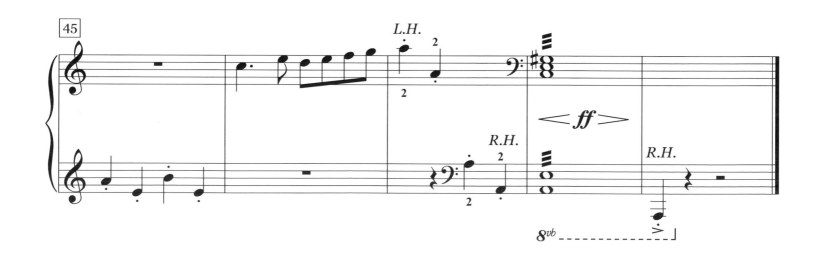

The Goblins

John Thompson

In a mysterious manner

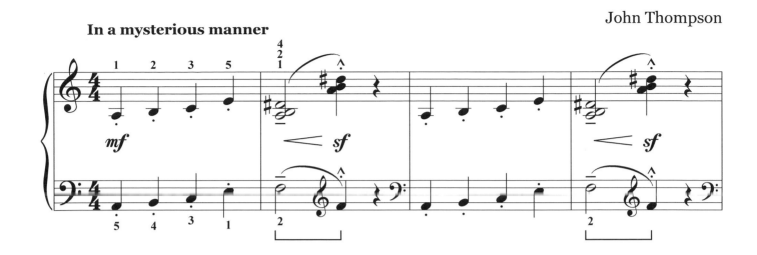

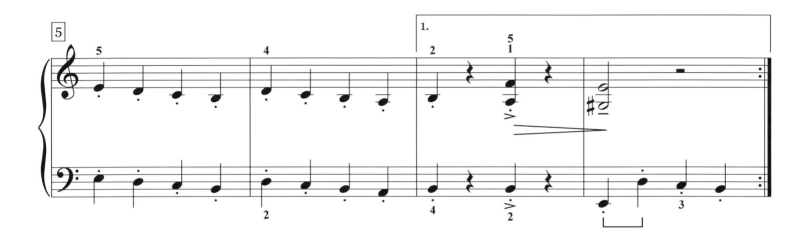

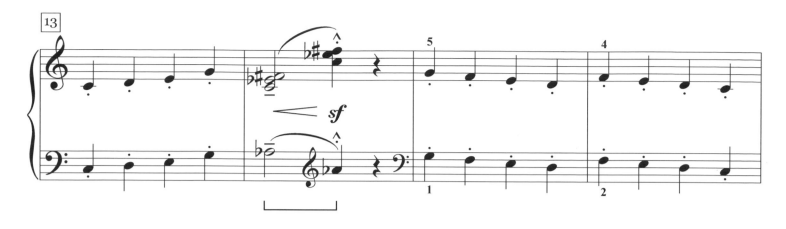

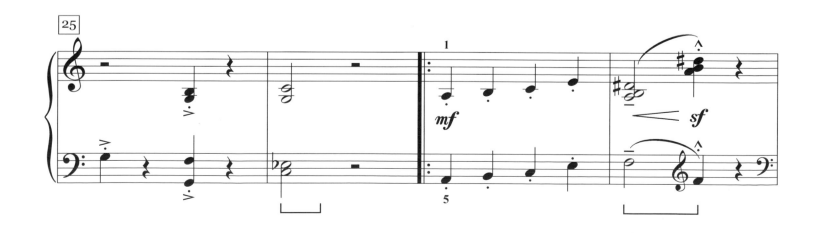

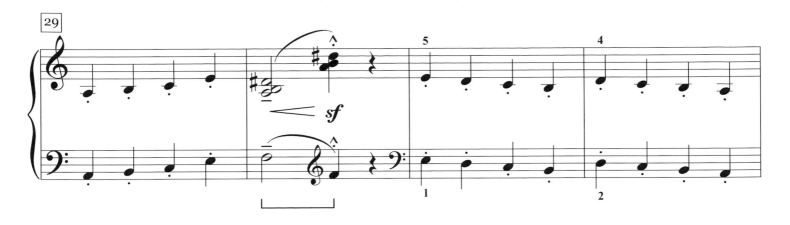

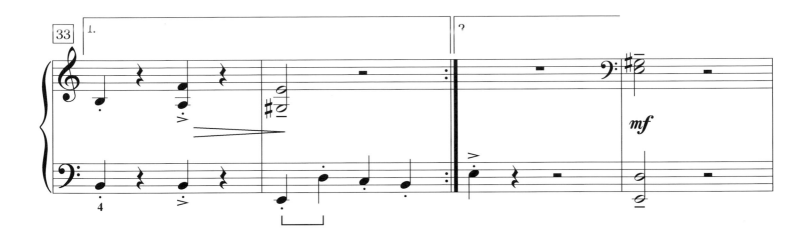

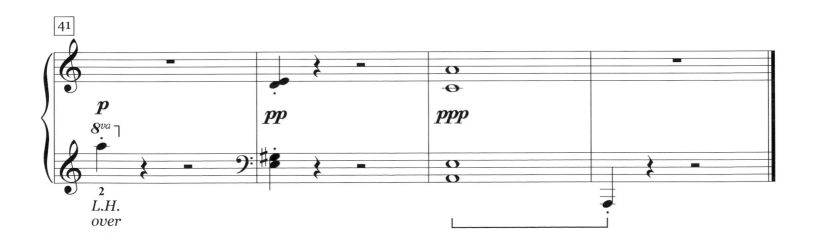

Creepy Crocodile

Carolyn C. Setliff

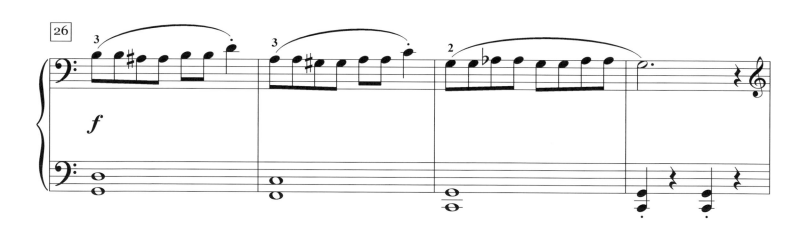

The Cool Skeleton

Carolyn Miller

* or other sound

19

Lupus Ululat

(Latin: *"the wolf howls"*)

Jason Sifford

From distant shadows ♩ = c. 108

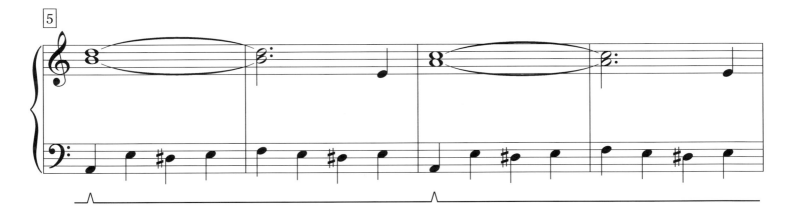

The chase begins! ♩ = c. 152

Into the Abyss

Charmaine Siagian

With an impending sense of doom ♩. = 78–90

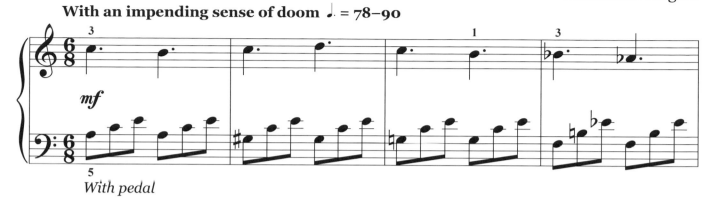

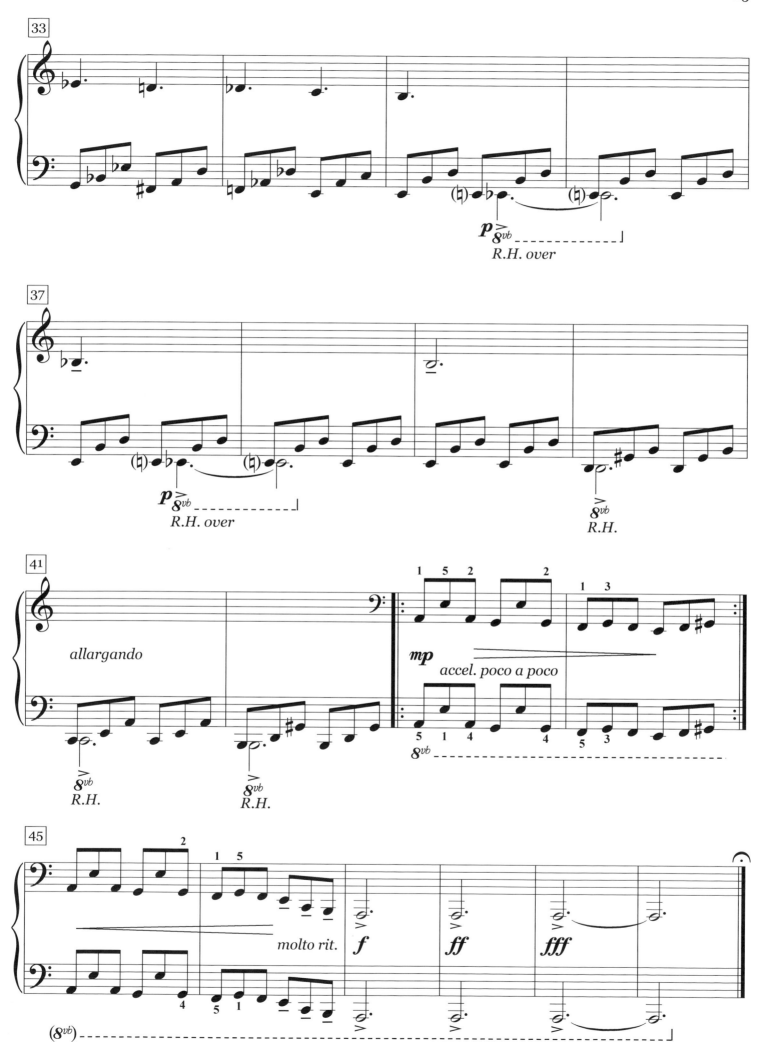

The Midnight Ball

Naoko Ikeda

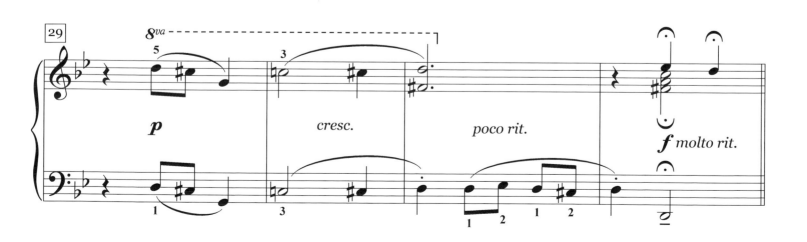

YOUR TURN

Can you come up with some strange sounds of your own on the piano?

PERFORMANCE NOTES

On This Eerie Night

This piece plays easy and sounds hard! Both the introduction and the codetta are in the Lydian mode. The melodic line is played by the right hand, in a single note pattern. Adding the pedal underneath the whole tone scale gives a lush harmonic sound. Listen to the slightly jazzy broken chord at the end; that's a C minor-major 7th! – *Glenda Austin*

Spooky Night

I call this a "one-page wonder," a piece accessible for most pianists with smaller hands. It introduces the ascending D melodic minor scale and opens the door for early ear training in distinguishing minor sounds. Gillock was a master of short, patterned solos that satisfy teacher, student, and listener. – *GA*

Escape from the Dark Forest

I always enjoy walks in the woods during the day. Nighttime is another story. There are dark shadows, rustling leaves, and unexpected sounds. Dramatic dynamic contrasts and clear articulation are essential elements to enhance this programmatic piece. Be sure to race the tempo at the ending so you and I can escape unharmed. Then we can share a good laugh. – *Randall Hartsell*

A Haunted House

Have you ever passed a big empty rundown mansion? This is the perfect piece to use your imagination about what goes on inside. – *CS*

The Goblins

Goblins are mythical creatures that appear in European folklore. They are often described as small and mischievous, so do your best to portray that character with short staccatos and theatrical *sf*s. Trivia: John Thompson had many pen names throughout his career. This piece was originally written under the name Edgar Belwood. – *CS*

Creepy Crocodile

Sneaking along, movin' to a beat | Ready to catch something good to eat!
Contrasting dynamics and clear staccatos will make this musical picture come alive. – *Carolyn C. Setliff*

The Cool Skeleton

Have fun with this piece! Measures 17–22 look difficult, but it's only the 2 black keys and 3 black key groupings played together. Keep the rhythm steady as you snap your fingers. Enjoy! – *Carolyn Miller*

Lupus Ululat

The word "ululat" is a great example of an onomatopoeia, a word that sounds like what it means. We hear the wolf howl "ar-ooo!" throughout the right hand part. In the fast part of the piece, imagine the beast racing through the underbrush in search of adventure! – *Jason Sifford*

Into the Abyss

On the island of Borneo is a craggy blue mountain that glistens in the sun. Hikers who make it all the way to the peak can peer over the edge to see a deep abyss enveloped in grey fog. As you play this piece, imagine a little stone tumbling over and over into the hidden darkness. Keep both hands legato and include some shrewd rubato throughout. – *Charmaine Siagian*

The Midnight Ball

There is a secret door to get to the Midnight Ball. A black cat with shiny eyes sits in front and only allows the most special guests in. You have been deemed important, along with elegant witches and clever ghosts who slip through walls and fly between silver chandeliers. There's a surprise in every room! Who will you invite to the ball? – *Naoko Ikeda*

ABOUT

GLENDA AUSTIN is an arranger and composer from Joplin, Missouri. During the 2020–21 pandemic she has been performing almost weekly on Facebook Live with the help of her husband David. She would love for you to follow her on YouTube.

EDNA MAE BURNAM (1907–2007) was born in California and authored the iconic Dozen a Day books. She learned piano from her mother, a piano teacher who drove her horse and buggy through the Sutter Buttes mountain range every day to reach students.

WILLIAM GILLOCK (1917–1993) grew up on a farm in rural Missouri. Art and music were the loves of his existence and many teachers throughout the world still refer to him as the "Schubert of children's composers."

RANDALL HARTSELL lives in Charlotte, North Carolina and is happily retired from teaching. He enjoys composing, biking, and gardening with his partner Ron.

NAOKO IKEDA is a teacher and composer who lives in Sapporo, a large city in northern Japan that is famous for its snow festivals. One of her favorite bands is the acapella group Take 6.

CAROLYN MILLER and her husband Gary live in Cincinnati, Ohio. She loves to teach and compose. The late great Regis Philbin once performed two of her pieces on national television!

CAROLYN C. SETLIFF is a teacher and composer from Little Rock, Arkansas. While not the biggest fan of technology, during the pandemic she mastered online teaching.

CHARMAINE SIAGIAN was born in Sabah, Malaysia and is editor of educational piano at Hal Leonard.

JASON SIFFORD lives in Iowa City, where he teaches a wonderful group of devoted students, performs regularly with immensely talented local artists, and composes music for his inner child. You can find Jason at **www.jasonsifford.com**.

JOHN THOMPSON (1889–1963) was the author of several landmark piano methods that continue to be bestsellers. Many teachers today studied from a Thompson book, yet are not aware that he composed intricate pieces at all levels. Thompson was also the director of the Conservatory of Music of Kansas City (now UMKC) from 1930–39.